Casey—
for being an
outstanding educator,
Thank You!
Joan
Parsons
Kurnitis

**"Look back to learn,
look forward to succeed."**

PEDAGOGY

Reflections on a Life Spent Learning

Joan Parsons Kuraitis

Ten|16
PRESS
www.TEN16press.com - Waukesha, WI

Pedagogy

Pedagogy by Joan Kuraitis
ISBN 978-1-64538-142-6

For information, please contact:

Ten 16 PRESS

www.TEN16press.com
Waukesha, WI

Cover design by Kaeley Dunteman

For

Grace
Luke
Adeline
and Charlie—

for all you have taught me.

TABLE OF CONTENTS

INTRODUCTION

Embarking on any new project fills me with a sense of renewed energy and hope, as I imagine the final product. It's an opportunity to express feelings, ideas, and wisdom, and make them permanent on paper. This book highlights some of the life lessons learned both in and out of the classroom, throughout my seven decades. From Pennsylvania (1952-70), Ohio (1970-84), Texas (1984-86), Illinois (1986-94), Iowa (1994-2014), and Wisconsin (2014-present), there have been many guideposts along the way populated by remarkable people who have enhanced my learning to a profound degree.

First, and foremost, I acknowledge my family of origin—father, mother, and two older sisters. Lessons learned at the dinner table over the years are still echoing in my head today. Childhood friends in the neighborhood, first cousins, and teachers in my grade school—they all helped form me in noticeable ways as well.

Special recognition is expressed to the teachers at Baker Elementary School in Altoona, Pennsylvania, for their guidance and strict boundaries in the classroom. Because of them, I pursued education as my life's work. Truly, those ladies of the 1950s and 1960s classrooms made all the difference in my life today.

Everyone takes away lessons from daily experiences. Be ready to learn from those experiences, be patient for answers, and above all listen. Messages present themselves as whispers at times, then smack us in the face if we are not paying attention. The following essays represent the most powerful lessons in my life to this point. I am not finished learning.

Joan Parsons Kuraitis
April, 2020

Part One

SCHOOL

PEDAGOGY

Pedagogy is the kind of word that sounds musical and rolls off the tongue easily and with conviction. Simply described, pedagogy is both the art and science of teaching. In short, it is the work of teachers. I consider myself a student of this profession and have been studying and practicing it all my life.

My informal education began in April of 1952, as the third and final daughter born to middle-class parents in central Pennsylvania. My mother fit the typical stereotype of homemakers in the 1950s, a version of Donna Reed or June Cleaver, the quintessential housewives of that decade. Later, in the 1960s she became a Mary Tyler Moore to her Dick Van Dyke—very stylish, very modern, and on point with the times, trends, and fashions. She made homemaking and mothering look like second nature. Vacuuming in classic cotton shirtwaist dresses or mastering a lengthy "to do" list each day appeared effortless. Mom was my first teacher of style, grace, and poise.

Formal education began for me in 1956 at the age of four. Together with my best buddy from across the street—Waggie Good, sandy-haired and blue-eyed—we attended private kindergarten in a church basement five mornings a week. Mrs. Hoffman—tall, lean, and grey-haired—provided an age-appropriate curriculum rich in play, singing, numbers, letters, colors, and clock reading. I completed the program two years later with a kindergarten certificate in hand and the assurance that I was ready for all-day first grade at Baker School, our neighborhood elementary school.

First grade was full of reading, reading, and more reading. I landed in the middle group in terms of ability, and I had to work hard to master the words and phrases in the Dick and Jane basal readers. See Dick. See Jane. See Dick run. See Jane run. It was drill and kill, but it certainly was effective. I will be forever grateful to my teacher Miss Little for her persistence. Without my constant practice on the Dick and Jane books, and without Miss Little's patience, I would never be the voracious reader I am today.

Throughout the elementary grades at Baker School, I experienced a succession of talented, but strict, teachers including Mrs. Merkel, Mrs. Eisenberg, Mrs. Laird, Miss Beck, and Miss Wilson. Each and every female instructor demonstrated both the art and science of teaching in ways that stayed with me throughout my life. Selecting education as my profession manifested as a tribute to every successful educator who modeled the highest standards of preparation, organization, and engagement possible to me in my lifetime.

Miss Beck stands alone as one of my favorite teachers. She taught fifth and sixth grade music class. In addition, she directed me in the children's choir at church where I participated from grades four through eight. Miss Beck gave life to the term music Ninja with her quick precision and efficiency. With an abundance of patience, she could coax a tune out of fifty restless grade school students and whip a Broadway-level show into place in four weeks. Miss Beck created a world where all things were beautiful. Having said that, my singing voice was not always beautiful, and certainly left room for improvement. On occasion, especially in our church choir setting, Miss Beck would remind me to "bring it down." Clearly, I was off key. Miss Beck revealed constructive criticism and critiques in such a pleasant way I never felt discouraged by her comments.

For my entire teaching career, I promoted the message to my students loud and clear: "I loved school so much, I never left." Choosing a profession is one of the most important decisions any individual will ever make in life. "Be thoughtful, be clear on your gifts, and remember that every job offers both rewards and setbacks."

The rewards in my profession became evident to me early in the game—I was learning right along with my students. I could actually get paid to continue my own education until retirement.

Throughout my career, I have taught in every grade level from kindergarten to graduate school. The privilege of teaching and learning encompass my time as a teacher, a substitute, a principal, and a college instructor. Of all these learning levels, five-year old students were my absolute favorites because they are capable of creating magic with nothing more than a few dolls to dress, a pile of Legos, or a sheet of colored construction paper and a box of Crayola

Crayons. Graduate students and seasoned educators were a close second for the brave way they managed large groups of diverse learners while presenting challenging instructional activities in the classroom. The beauty of teaching, for me, will always be learning.

Now, since my retirement, as the long, light-filled days of summer give way to the cool, crisp air of fall, I turn my attention to the classroom once again. For well over sixty years, I have been part of a school setting. This year is no different. Formal education continues for me as a student of writing and French. This is a new school year, and so begins a new collection of memories, all added to the long list of reflections on a life spent learning.

THE DESK

Before

In 1960, the world as my family knew it was about to be turned upside down. The Vietnam War smoldered a world away, the civil rights movement gained traction and support across the country, and a handsome young man with a New England accent showed strength in the polls for the presidency. In spite of the changes in the wind, my rock-solid dad, with conservative values, continued to drive his reliable American-made Chevrolet each and every day. In spite of the troubled times elsewhere, my world continued to thrive on a steady diet of peace and predictability.

By the start of third grade in September of 1960, there appeared a new blond mid-century child's desk in my tiny bedroom. Sleek and simple, the desk's purpose was to provide me with a much-needed quiet spot for homework, for thinking, and for dreaming. The desk was all that, and more.

In third grade, with little or no homework, I used the desktop to "iron" my stack of cotton handkerchiefs just as I perceived my mom doing at her ironing board in the basement each week. A small cup of water from the bathroom plus a comb became the tools of my trade that year. In the late afternoon, the hour just before dinner, I proceeded to pretend to iron the hankies with water and a smooth surface provided by the back of the comb. I folded and stacked the neat pile of cotton squares, a job that kept me occupied and modeled how I perceived my mom working at her ironing board. I created that job myself.

By seventh grade, I felt challenged by the homework—especially in science, a subject I never could grasp. I sat for hours at my desk and read the pages of my textbook aloud in my tiny room, hoping to absorb the content if I saw it and heard the words. I struggled to learn science that year, but managed to pull out a B for the course.

Eighth grade provided a new use for the desk. By the time I reached the age of thirteen in 1965, sewing ignited my imagination. My mother spent her reserves of cash one month to buy me a used sewing machine, and I went to town. First I made skirts, then jumpers, and finally accomplished more advanced work on dresses. My little desk, with its scattered pins and tissue-paper pattern pieces, served as the space I needed to sew on a machine and create clothing for school. My schoolwork space promptly moved to the adjacent twin bed.

In late summer of 1966, I graduated to my older sister's bedroom with the twin beds and coveted private bathroom. Clearly, I was grown up and no longer in need of the room everyone continued referring to as "the baby room." No more tiny room for me. No more tiny furniture. No more working at my favorite space.

My simple blond wood desk and matching adjustable chair were relocated to the basement of our home in Pennsylvania. For the next five decades, the desk and chair languished in basements or garages of residences in Pennsylvania, Ohio, Texas, Illinois, Iowa, and Wisconsin.

After

Happily, the desk and chair have been refurbished and are now flourishing in the bedroom of my young granddaughter, Grace. This kind, smart, and serious student received my cherished desk on the occasion of her sixth birthday in 2015. Grace uses her desk almost everyday for thinking, writing, and dreaming. It makes a quiet comfortable spot for her to imagine the future. My heart is filled with joy as this solid symbol of studying and creating enjoys a new life back in the state of Ohio once again.

MISS WILSON

Baker School

Sixth grade at Baker School ranks as my all-time favorite year of education. It was the fall of 1963 and Miss Wilson, a seasoned veteran in the classroom, knew just how to handle her four most eager students—Nancy, Barb, Virginia, and me. We all lived in the same neighborhood, and with the exception of Virginia, our token redhead, we all sported stylish brunette bobs.

Our classroom was located in the original section of the school building with well-worn oak flooring faded to a pale orange/yellow, and large sash windows with aged, chipping frames that allowed light to stream into the room at all hours of the morning or afternoon. The room certainly showed signs of wear and tear. My two older sisters experienced this room, as did my mother more than two decades earlier.

Miss Wilson, middle-aged and roundish with her simple attire of dark plaid shirtwaist dresses and sturdy shoes, was always prepared to teach. She kept a strict classroom schedule but allowed for some freedom of exploration among students. For example, the popular self-paced SRA reading program put students on an honor system and encouraged them to make progress individually. The problem with that approach was that each reader picked a story suited to his or her reading level (how is one supposed to know?), read the story, and answered comprehension questions. Each set of questions also included the answers on the back of the card. With 26 independent readers in class each morning, it likely meant some peeking at answers occurred. I am still not convinced that my reading skills improved that year, but I managed to wrangle a set of straight A's in sixth grade.

As an added bonus, Miss Wilson trusted my three best friends—Nancy, Barb, Virginia—and me to be helpers in the first-grade classroom while Miss Moore, our school principal and first grade teacher did her administrative duties outside of the classroom part of the morning or afternoon. The four of us would proudly leave class on cue, dash down the long flight of stairs to the first floor, and share the oral reading duties with the first graders several days each week. Such a thrill to be released from class during the tedious SRA reading hour, with boring stories, and delight in reading to the first graders age-appropriate picture books about talking bunnies and friendly mice.

For extra credit, Miss Wilson selected the four of us to design and execute elaborate bulletin boards for the benefit of the entire class. One unit we covered in social studies included the history of Mexico. Again, our small group of four separated from the other students as we hashed out ideas, consulted encyclopedias, and sketched people for our Mexico mural. It was great fun and took nearly five days to complete. In the end, we had something that represented a typical modern-day marketplace on the streets of Mexico City. We approached the assignment with great enthusiasm, and it showed in our festive and colorful display.

In addition to our daily focus on academic subjects that year, all of the sixth grade girls, by tradition, were assigned to patrol the halls of the school four times a day—morning arrival, lunch dismissal, after lunch arrival, and end-of-day dismissal. When we were on duty, this added activity took us out of the classroom for an extra 40 minutes per day. The job was especially fun as we talked and giggled in the vast open halls of the building.

Our final privilege that year as the oldest students in the school, was to walk to the little pizza shop near the building on Friday afternoons. Instead of the usual lunch at home, our mothers agreed that we were mature enough to handle the added responsibility of lunch on our own. As pre-teens, the new Friday routine proved special and arrived at the perfect time—spring of our sixth grade year when we were all closing in on 12 years of age. Nancy, Barb, Virginia and I devoured our greasy pepperoni pizza, washed it down with ice-cold bottles of Coca-Cola or Orange Crush, and played a few rounds on a vintage pinball machine. The lunch break flew by quickly, and before long we gathered our coats and headed back to school.

Oh, the laughter and the pleasures of being 12 years old again! Never again would the four of us be in the same classroom. We entered junior high school along with students from several other grade schools in the fall of 1964. Everything was different. Now, our position was the very bottom of the food chain. We were peons as we made our way from classroom to classroom on a strict bell schedule every hour. No longer were we together all day. Forget about eating lunch at the same time, and no more Miss Wilson to divide the extra privileges among her four most trusted female students.

During the junior high school years, Virginia moved out of state with her family when her father accepted a new job, and we lost touch. Nancy lives in California. Barb resides in Pittsburgh and I live in the Milwaukee area. When I visit my old hometown of Altoona, Pennsylvania, every few years, I still see Barb and her mother, a lovely lady in her mid nineties.

MRS. BROWN

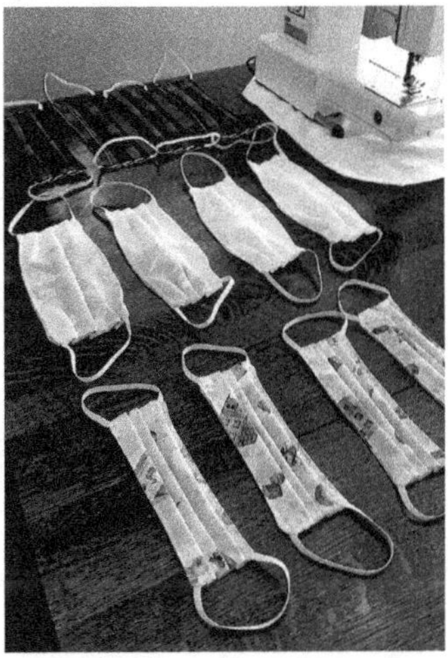

Putting sewing skills to use in 2020

Spring of 1966 in central Pennsylvania awakened with the blossoming of bright yellow forsythia bushes growing wild in our back yard. That April, I found myself in Mrs. Brown's sewing class at Theodore Roosevelt Junior High School for a full quarter. The curriculum included mastering two simple pillowcases, an apron, and an A-line skirt. My skirt was bright yellow, like the blooming flowers in my back yard.

Mrs. Brown, our middle-aged and soft-spoken teacher with grey hair piled high on her head who frequently peered up from her reading glasses, fit the bill of someone who loved to sew. She quietly explained directions, gave us measurements to follow, and assigned us to workstations in an effort to create and stitch usable garments. The work was engaging for me as a first-time sewer, and I often finished quickly, in time to assist a friend or two with their measuring and stitching.

Throughout the quarter, the projects were simple and basic, well suited to our eighth-grade group of novice female seamstresses. I never imagined as a young teen that this skill would stay with me for the next fifty plus years, and how grateful I would feel to have learned to sew from Mrs. Brown, our patient and proficient classroom leader. Her love of sewing would inspire me to try newer and more difficult tasks throughout my life.

After my years of making school outfits in junior high, high school, and college, I packed away my sewing machine for a full decade. Although it moved with me from Pennsylvania to Ohio, I put the hobby on hold as I juggled work, graduate school, and babies.

When my second baby girl arrived in 1982, the sewing began again in earnest with construction of infant garments and alterations to hand-me-down clothing from her older sister. By the age of seven in 1989, that daughter flatly pronounced: "I don't want homemade clothes anymore. I want to shop at The GAP."

Years passed and I used my sewing skills to create quilts and other crafts to decorate our home. I loved doing quick projects with the sewing machine and fabric such as doll clothes and pillows. Later, as a grandmother, I crafted appliqued lamb quilts for each grandbaby—two girls (2009 and 2012) and two boys (2010 and 2012), with the last baby arriving eight years ago.

In April 2020, during the time of coronavirus, my aging machine (well over 35 years old) was used in a new way, to create facemasks for family and neighbors. Quick and easy patterns appeared online. On a free Sunday afternoon, I cut and stitched a pile of masks and posted a photo to social media. One Facebook friend and former sewing classmate from my junior high days wrote on my page: "Mrs. Brown would be proud ."

MR. NIXON

Mr. Nixon strode into class each morning eager to teach. He was young and handsome, in a John Kennedy way. Fresh out of college, he walked a fine line of being our leader, yet understanding our interests with music, sports, and films. He even noticed if someone entered class with a new haircut or glasses, and he made sure to acknowledge those changes in a positive way.

Mr. Nixon was one of those memorable teachers you never forget. The academic year opened in September of 1969. My final year at Altoona High School would be one of my favorites. Upon the recommendation of my high school guidance counselor, I added a full year of Speech to my course schedule along with Senior English, Advanced Algebra, Biology, and Spanish III. Speech, as it turned out, was just what the name implied—a full year of writing, rehearsing, and delivering speeches of all genres.

From day one, our small class comprised of only seniors waited nervously for the direction of our new young teacher on how to present the most gut twisting of all deliveries—the demonstration speech. It seemed a little too personal for my shy self to reveal an actual skill to an entire class of peers. I elected to perform CPR since I recently earned certification by the Red Cross and passed the life guarding course in late summer. With the assistance of a good-natured classmate named Scott, I proceeded to demonstrate life-saving techniques to our small yet attentive group.

Our joyful young teacher with sandy blond hair and blue eyes was a one-of-a-kind educator for our one-of-a-kind class of seniors that year at Altoona

High School. With Scott, Barb (my sixth grade friend from Miss Wilson's class), Janet, Michele, Lind, and others, we all conquered our nerves and moved through life with added understanding of how to present ourselves to others—hands at sides, no filler words, and always giving eye contact.

On other occasions, Mr. Nixon asked us to prepare a poetry reading from memory. My favorite poet at the time was Robert Frost, and my reading included the gentle words from "Stopping By Woods On A Snowy Evening." By first drawing a deep breath, I delivered the most haunting lines in a slow, drawn-out manner for dramatic effect as I recited:

The woods are lovely, dark and deep.
But I have promises to keep.
And miles to go before I sleep.
And miles to go before I sleep.

From the beginning of the school year, I always sensed that we were Mr. Nixon's favorite students. Our instructor showed noticeable enthusiasm, sincere interest, and boundless energy in the classroom each day. Toward the end of the year, Mr. Nixon even arranged for us to play softball at a local park the last week of school, just to enjoy a final bonding experience before we all pursued separate life paths. Although I made an appearance with my friend Barb, I preferred to observe as the boys participated. Secretly, I believed Mr. Nixon used that outing as a way to spend time with our class, and his girlfriend . . . or was she his fiancée? Not sure how deeply they were involved at the time. All I remember is that my girlfriends and I were somewhat disappointed. Mr. Nixon had a life outside of school? Shocking!

Many years later at a high school reunion, Scott revealed that he had stayed in touch with Mr. Nixon over the years since graduation. Mr. Nixon left Altoona to pursue another teaching position in State College, Pennsylvania. I have thought of Mr. Nixon over the years, and wished him well in my head, but I never made the effort to contact him to explain how much I learned in my senior year of high school. He taught me poise, confidence, and an educator's professional demeanor—valuable lessons emphasized only in speech class.

Part Two

FAMILY LESSONS

IF YOU CAN'T SAY SOMETHING NICE...

Every adult in my generation clearly understands the message "If you can't say something nice, don't say anything at all." That directive, more than others, seemed to be drilled into my head by a mother who made it her goal each day to protect the feelings of others. So, with caution and a deep breath, I always tried to select my words carefully as a child or forego responding, especially in challenging situations.

From a very clever aunt many years after the fact, I learned that not all babies are beautiful or worthy of a Gerber print ad. When faced with the explosion of babies after World War II as men returned to their wives at home, this aunt might have been found saying with a demure smile, "now that's a baby" when introduced to a friend's new offspring. Clearly, that baby did not have the qualities, or appearance, to rank among the most cherubic of infants.

My mother had her own version of that message. For example, if one of my friends showed up at school with a choppy new haircut, she taught me to say, "You got a haircut" and nothing more. Permanents and hair dye were all subject to hideous results in the 1950s and 1960s, but my mother showed much restraint and kindness when saying to her friends "That style looks good on you."

My father's approach to the adage of saying something nice followed him into his profession as a realtor. Over the course of his career, he met hundreds of homeowners, both buyers and sellers. Although my dad had specific and freakishly high standards for maintaining a house, he held his tongue until he arrived home promptly at 5:45 each evening, and unloaded an earful to my mother as she quickly put the finishing touches on our six o'clock dinner. I overheard his true feelings about every one of his clients and their skills at home maintenance. My mother, however, presented her core values of kindness, graciousness, and inclusiveness to the world, making her the diplomat of the family. At least Dad was careful in his professional life.

Recently, I presented a book titled Simpatico about my mother to the world. While most people have been positive, one comment stands out to me from a reader who said, when probed, "Oh, you wrote a book." While I can understand the reader sticking to the adage "don't say anything at all" it felt like the comment "Now that's a baby." Admittedly, I'm a little dampened by the reader's comment, but I also understand that peoples' tastes vary. For the most part, people have been enthusiastic and complimentary in their remarks to me, and I very much appreciate that the work is well received by my closest circle of family and friends.

In life, we are all challenged by on-the-spot responses to questions and revelations. Are we prepared to pull a neutral comment out of our arsenal of responses so as to protect the feelings of the person in our company? The message still resonates in my heart and mind, and in the calm voice of my mother: "Joanie, if you can't say something nice, don't say anything at all." Words to live by.

DINNERTIME LECTURES

Joan's Father

America in the 1950s flourished under the leadership of President Dwight D. Eisenhower, our 34th Chief Executive. Perhaps it was Eisenhower's military experience as a general in World War II or the hero worship my parents felt for this man, but my dad actually governed his family on the same principles as a small platoon. Clearly, Dad was the officer just as he had been in the Navy during the Second World War, and my mother and we three daughters just followed orders.

Each night at our grey Formica dinner table with the aroma of broiled lamb chops filling our tiny kitchen, my dad enlightened us with his pearls of wisdom. As a quiet child, I listened more than I ever spoke, so the lectures were perfect for me. As I advanced in age, I absorbed more of the meanings in these messages, and allowed them to permeate my soul.

Here's what I learned at the dinner table in the 1950s and 1960s, right through my teen years. First and foremost, never complain about your job. Since I was just a kid, that message fell on deaf ears for a very long time, but nevertheless it did sink into my being. As I matured, I was grateful for work that guaranteed a paycheck. Secondly, Dad promoted a message of hard work. "Be at work early, and always stay late," he professed. "Do more than your supervisor asks of you." It took time for this message to sink in, but it did eventually become part of my DNA in the work setting.

Lessons about money came down like this: "Save, save, save." From the age of five, I had been saving my allowance, which was only 50 cents per week, enough to fund my movie ticket for a double feature on Saturday and buy popcorn and candy. If I chose to forego the Saturday movie with neighborhood friends, I could double my savings by the following week. My meager stash of cash proved useful, as it bailed my mom out of a few tight financial situations by Friday evening, the end of her own "allowance" week. She needed to pay the paper delivery boy before my dad arrived home from work. Saving is still my major method of operation—although now I am in the golden years of life and know the pattern of behavior should switch to spending. I'm still getting used to that way of living.

Dad also had conservative ideas about male chauvinism. He made proclamations like this: "Girls, all you have in life is your reputation." Not sure what he wanted me to do with those words until much later. When I was eight, he calmly directed me to remember that it is a man's world, and men like sports. Therefore, I should learn to love sports. That comment alone made me bristle at the idea of being considered a second-class citizen in my own family.

Also learned at the dinner table in my youth was how to appraise a house. Since my father spent his career as a realtor—and a mighty good one at that—he was always quizzing us girls on the value of houses in Altoona, Pennsylvania. I learned how square footage translates to the value of a property. In addition, I came to realize that an in-ground pool and pets devalue a house and the land upon which it sits. New kitchens and bathrooms sell a house. I learned these lessons as a grade school child.

Dinner table experiences these days might feel a little different in families. Some talk politics, some impart lessons like my childhood family, and some sit in front of the TV and don't talk at all. For me, I still enjoy mealtime conversation around a few tasty dishes, especially when we laugh about the past, and share dreams about the future.

MOTHER'S RULES FOR DRESSING

Mother looking picture perfect

Long ago it became clear to me that there are specific rules for dressing. As a young girl observing my mother prepare for outings, I learned the unwritten rules for dressing. She might have been preparing for Sunday morning at church, or something much fancier requiring a long dress and her finest jewels. I soaked in all of her preparations as if studying for final exams at school.

Over the course of about 12 to 14 years, the timeframe in which I showed an interest in watching my mother prepare to go out, I was mesmerized by the time and attention she devoted to her "look" that evening. While observing from the end of her bed, I watched as she carefully fixed her hair, applied mascara and bright red lipstick, and selected her undergarments in a most thoughtful manner. The final touch was a few drops of Shalimar perfume. That sweet scent still lingers in my nose today.

In a quiet, unspoken way, my mother taught me to follow a few simple rules for dressing. Always stick to solid colors—they are much classier than busy prints. Buy tailored dresses that fit well and flatter your figure. Avoid trendy clothes; obviously, they go out of style in a year or two and are not a good investment. Wear classic pearls whenever you dress up for a special event such as weddings, funerals, garden parties, and ladies' teas. Avoid white after Labor Day and before Memorial Day.

My mother's hard and fast rules about fashion required that shoes and purses match in color and leather. Always remember to dress for the occasion, and it's better to show up overdressed rather than underdressed. Those were clearly words to live by, even today in our much more casual society. For the most part, my sisters and I followed our mother's rules for many, many years.

Recently, while sorting a box of old photos, I happened upon a picture taken in Florida in 1984 depicting my mother, my sister, and me, each of us cleaned, polished, and styled to go out to dinner. We all dressed separately that evening, then gathered together for a photo to document the occasion. There we stood as three clones of one another in light silky blue dresses with sleeves and our finest pearls. Clearly, we all graduated from the same school of dressing—Mother's school.

GRANDMA PARSONS

My Grandma Parsons championed education, hard work, and religion. Grandma Parsons, or Helen Kantner Parsons to her friends and family, was an inspiration to those who knew her best. Her core values must have been learned long ago from her parents. Today, the lessons learned from Grandma Parsons have been passed down through the generations from me to my own children and grandchildren.

Helen Kantner was born in Altoona, Pennsylvania in 1889—the year of the unveiling of the Eiffel Tower in Paris at the tenth Exposition Universelle. Technology and architecture were cutting edge sciences in that period. However, I wonder how Altoona looked—and smelled—in the late 1800s. The railroad industry was booming, and Altoona was fortunate enough to be a hub for rail car repairs, and transfers to all locations north, east, south, and west. The scent of burning coal permeated the homes of residents both near and far from the downtown train station.

Helen met and married Chester Parsons, joining their lives together in 1910 at the age of 21 for Helen and 24 for Chester. They raised a family of four healthy children, all born at home. The oldest child Thomas was born in 1913, followed by Helen in 1915, William in 1917, and Frances in 1924.

Helen Kantner Parsons must have imparted strong values of education and religion since all four children graduated from Duke University in Durham, North Carolina. From the mid 1800s onward, Duke adopted the motto "Knowledge and Religion." Perhaps that was the key component that drew my grandmother, a girl with only an eighth-grade education, to the small southern Methodist institution for all four of her children.

The oldest, Tom, was an exceptional student and athlete who supported himself in college on scholarships and work-study jobs. My father Bill did the same thing, excelling in academics, basketball, and tennis. Bill was the captain of Duke's basketball team from 1939 to 1940. He supported himself in college on scholarships and work-study jobs just as his brother before him. The sisters Helen and Frances worked their way through college as well.

Brothers Tom and Bill succeeded in business, taking over Parsons Agency for Real Estate and Insurance, founded by their father in 1920. The business thrived, especially in the 1960s and 1970s. The sisters were successful in their own way as well. Helen married a businessman and raised four children while volunteering in her community of State College, Pennsylvania, a prosperous college town. Frances pursued a career in occupational therapy, eventually working as the head of the department at Cleveland Clinic while raising two children of her own.

For my dear Grandma Parsons, my first role model of a church lady, I learned to love baking, sewing, and all things related to church such as Sunday school, vacation bible school, ladies' meetings, and choir. In the process, I do believe that my grandmother's passion for higher education penetrated my being as well. She never expected her daughters to do anything less than her sons did after college. They never disappointed Grandma Parsons.

SUMMER ROAD TRIPS

Northern Wisconsin

No one loved a road trip more than my father. He was the king of the road with his expert driving skills, cruising in his blue four-door Chevy sedan each summer as all five of us piled our luggage into the car and headed from central Pennsylvania to the Jersey Shore. The July weather was consistently hot and humid as we drove on highways and byways, absorbing the thick stale air as it melted my sisters and me in the back seat of Dad's road beast. We were on our way to our annual summer beach vacation and air conditioning did not exist.

Gingy, my oldest sister, amused herself by polishing her fingernails on her small, hard-shell cosmetics bag, balanced with great concentration on her two skinny knees. Georgia, the middle sister, insisted on picking the radio station—and top 40 music—much to my Dad's annoyance. And I was crammed into the middle back seat with no window or fresh air to soothe me during those endless hours in the car. Typical family fun in the 1950s!

Years later, when I was a parent and very aware of the comforts of home while traveling by car, I allowed my daughter Anne to make a bed out of the far back bench of our minivan in the 1980s. Anne loaded the car with blankets, pillows, books, music, food, and drinks. She wanted for nothing on our ten-hour drives from Illinois to Pennsylvania. Skipping the seat belt may not have been the safest way to travel, but Anne was quiet and comfortable during those many long hours in the car.

Now, our road trips are geared strictly for adults. My husband and I are road warriors in our long excursions both in America and abroad. For example, in August of 2018, my husband, our daughters, and I navigated Lithuania, a country adjacent to the Baltic Sea about half the size of Wisconsin. With nothing more than our rental car and an iPhone map app, we traveled with confidence while touring historic landmarks, ancient graveyards, tourist attractions, and the personal residence of my husband's first cousin. The trip was a rare gift of time and experience as we united as a nuclear family of four, once again.

Also included in our recent road trips was an excursion around the state of Wisconsin. My husband and I made multiple stops, including the state capital of Madison and the weekend farmers' market. Personally, I enjoyed La Crosse, with its scenic Granddad Bluff, and lazy Mississippi River views. Spooner and Hayward made the cut and merited a stop to visit a new friend for lunch. After soaking in the beauty of Lake Superior, we traveled on to Door County to gaze upon the orange and pink sunsets over Green Bay. We made it back home in a week after circling the entire state of Wisconsin. That trip will always be one of my favorites.

Road trips are a unique way to travel—slow enough to take in the scenery, economical, and full of unplanned adventures. When I'm yearning for a getaway (usually in the dead of winter), I think of summer road trips with open highways, local food, sites to explore, and one-of-a-kind shopping.

Lessons from childhood, although similar to a spoonful of castor oil at times, might just create the favorite memories of all. Road trips practiced over time and learned the hard way, are still my favorite way to spend a summer week in the Midwest.

Part Three

WORK

FROM STUDENT TO TEACHER IN SIXTY SECONDS

Joan's first year of teaching

When does anyone know the exact moment they cross that subtle, imperceptible line separating two distinct worlds—that of the adult and that of the almost-adult? My moment occurred at the age of 21 on my first paid assignment as a classroom teacher. The year was 1973 in Cuyahoga Falls, a suburb of industrial Akron.

Eager to get married and start a new life in another state with my husband, I accelerated my bachelor's degree program and finished four years of coursework, with a dual major and two quarters of student teaching in three years. At that time in my life, I was highly motivated to move to the next level both personally and professionally. By the time I turned 21, I had a college diploma in hand with initials B.S.Ed. behind my name, and that all-important "Mrs." in front.

Entering my profession in Ohio as a teacher of special needs students, the school district assigned me to a high school classroom as a substitute teacher in a program for delayed learners. Some of my students told me they were 21 years of age. Surveying the classroom before the first bell rang, I was drawn to a petite girl with dark curly hair who openly proclaimed that she was 21. Due to several retentions along the way from kindergarten to her senior year in high school, she had reached the legal age for drinking while still a high school student.

Also present in my class of seniors was a very large young man, easily outweighing me by a good hundred pounds, towering over me in a very noticeable way. (I stand five feet seven inches in my socks.) That gentle giant was also my age, and proud to share that information with me.

That sweet, delicate little girl and the towering hulk were definitely the extremes in an otherwise normal-looking class of adolescents. Every student in that classroom had endured retentions over the years, and it was a bit unnerving to know these students were so close to my own age. At the sound of the first bell, I sucked in my breath, smoothed my baby blue polyester pantsuit, and transformed from student to teacher in 60 seconds.

Instantly my thinking shifted, and my role became the confident adult in charge of a classroom full of high-need students. With the training I received in special education and the status of being married, I knew I was light years apart from my students in real world experience. Would those few extra years of training and my married status suffice in seeing me through the whole day or week with a diverse group of young learners ranging in ability and size, from the most under developed girls to the huskiest of boys? The answer was a resounding YES!

I conquered my fear and insecurity the day I managed my first class of students, many of whom were taller and more mature looking than I. Once they became comfortable calling me "Mrs. Kuraitis," my own lack of self-confidence melted into the natural rhythm of teaching, often referred to as "flow" by seasoned professionals. My foray into the world of grownups required an ability to command the classroom, deliver course content in reading and math, and memorize the schedules of 15 students, each with entirely different work-study assignments for part of the day.

I believe this old adage to be true: "Life does not throw you more than you can handle." Without a doubt, my confidence grew enormously during that teaching assignment. For me, the opportunity to challenge myself as an educator while maintaining a standard of friendly professionalism was the first genuine lesson in how to function as an adult.

Today, I am happily retired after 33 years of experience as an educator. The rewards of teaching far outweighed anything I might have encountered in another profession. The years passed quickly, and gave me great insight in all grade levels from kindergarten to graduate coursework for teachers.

The fearlessness originating from those first days of teaching in the early 1970s now allows me to tackle new assignments and projects in all types of conditions. I see this trait as a gift practiced in those very first days of my teaching career. And, for this gift, I am genuinely grateful.

LEARNING ON THE JOB

Joan as a first-year principal.

What does it take to fill the shoes of a Catholic School principal when your professional experience has never placed you in that position in the past? As a convert to Roman Catholicism a mere decade prior, surely there was something lacking in my training to follow in the footsteps of some very accomplished nuns and lay educators in my adopted state of Iowa more than 20 years ago.

This seed of an idea to pursue the lead position in a small Catholic school in Davenport had its inception in a casual conversation over cocktails at a local Catholic fundraiser in the spring of 1996. Still fairly new to Iowa, I was learning the ropes about the local schools, teacher qualifications, and certification procedures in the area. Here's how the conversation unfolded over cold drinks that evening in the vast Assumption High School gymnasium:

Church Acquaintance #1: "Did you know that Sacred Heart is looking for a new principal? You should apply."

Joan: "I'm not certified to be a principal."

Church Acquaintance #1: "That's OK. Apply anyway."

Later that evening, I ran into another acquaintance at the gathering. Our conversation unfolded in an eerily similar manner.

Church Acquaintance #2: "Did you know that Lourdes is looking for a new principal? You should apply."

Joan: "I'm not certified to be a principal."
Church Acquaintance #2: "That's OK. Apply anyway."

At that point, I was beginning to think the state of Iowa had completely different requirements for educators working as administrators. Maybe I was just uninformed on the procedures for this type of certification. In spite of those thoughts, and with the echo of the two ladies' casual comments at the party still ringing in my mind, I threw my hat in the ring the very next week and applied for work as a Catholic school principal in eastern Iowa.

Apparently, I was the candidate who looked most like a nun because the interviews produced a job offer. As luck would have it, I was selected to lead Sacred Heart Cathedral School, the smallest and poorest of the Catholic schools in the area. Just a few years before, the parish priest conducted passive marches and demonstrations to rid the neighborhood of drug dealers and other illegal businesses. His efforts proved successful and that little school began to attract new families.

The first few months on the job, my husband always made sure to ask me, "How was work today?" or, "How do you know what to do each day?"

How does anyone work as a principal when there has been no direct training for that job? Years of observation would be my best answer. Anyone can learn any skill by observing, processing, and trying. That was my mode of operation each and every day. Show up early, work long and hard, and rely on skills observed in the past from successful veteran principals. In addition, there is the need to follow one's core values when making decisions.

Does this help our teachers perform at a higher level?
Will this assist students in achieving better results in the classroom?
Can the school afford something new and innovative?
Am I following the doctrine of the Catholic Church?

Truly, that first year was all about learning on the job. Discipline was the most challenging situation of all. Yes, there was a disciplinary policy in place, but the students presented clever, fresh, and unexpected challenges on a daily basis. For example—one year on Halloween, I dressed as my daughter in her high school varsity volleyball uniform, kneepads included.

Later that afternoon, I was summoned by a classroom teacher to the junior high school bathroom on the second floor to deal with a few 12-year-old boys who clogged the toilets with paper towels just for fun. As we were walking to my office for a little chat, I kept wondering to myself, "Will these boys take me seriously? I'm wearing a costume." Of course, they took me seriously, and the matter was resolved in about 15 minutes. That afternoon, those spirited boys learned a critical life lesson that involved rubber gloves, bleach, and a plunger.

Mishaps and missteps resolved themselves on a daily basis that first year as a principal. We proceeded with our lives as educators and students in our little school on East 12th Street and LeClaire Avenue in Davenport, Iowa. Over the years, though, it became crystal clear to me that, in fact, experience is the best teacher. Learning on the job allows for professional growth, problem solving, and satisfaction that endures well beyond the boundaries of the professional position.

WHY HOMEWORK MATTERS

Homework is the work assigned by a teacher for his or her students to complete outside the classroom. The work can take the form of additional practice such as with math facts or weekly spelling words. As students grow, the assignments might include something much larger in scope, such as a five-page research paper that requires finding reliable sources and additional outside reading separate from the class.

As a lifelong learner, I learned to love school at a very young age. If our class had no homework, I would create homework or play school after spending the past seven hours in my formal classroom. The activities I did to reinforce learning at home included writing my weekly spelling words over and over to perfect the order of the letters as well as the printing, and later, cursive formations. I loved math, so practicing math facts became second nature for me. It was fun and challenging to spit out the answers as fast as my mother could turn the flashcards in her hands. In social studies, I always created colorful poster boards to present to my class on states we were studying at that time. Bright collages became my trademark style for presenting new information.

When my daughters were in grade school, we always prioritized finishing homework right after school, before playing games indoors or out. There was never conflict over finishing schoolwork on time, and in a very neat hand. Both girls understood the value of completing work as soon as the teacher assigned it, and with a high standard of quality.

In my own teaching experience, I heard the gambit of excuses for why homework was not completed on time and with care. For example, the common response to unfinished or missing homework sounded like this:

"My mother did not put it in my backpack last night."

To that simple comment, I replied: "It was not your mother's job to load your backpack." Everything from "The dog ate my work" to "The hamster got loose last night and chewed my papers" became the rhythm of life in the classroom each morning. I listened with patience and regrouped to ensure the student still learned the valuable lessons with practice opportunities in that lost homework assignment.

Here's what I know for sure about homework: If you train children to believe that school is their job, they may take homework seriously. If you provide a quiet space for work with good lighting and no clutter to distract them, they may complete their work on time. And if you take the time to proofread their work and provide helpful suggestions for improvement, they learn the high standards that are expected by their classroom teacher.

Homework is important and does matter as some of the first training a child receives in life. If done right, homework provides the foundation for discipline, punctuality, and neatness. Managing time and resources is a very important life skill to be learned and practiced for the rest of our lives. Start early, assist students when needed, and support their efforts to improve.

In today's world, homework has become a controversial topic for discussion among parents, teachers, and administrators. Whether the work is completed in school or at home, everyone needs to understand that it's part of the learning process, and it is practice that goes toward learning and mastery.

Here is my recommendation for the modern world: Lengthen the school day. Make it a full eight hours from start to finish, let's say 8 AM to 4 PM. At the end of each instructional day, students have the opportunity to finish all left over work from the day, with the assistance of the teacher to oversee the work. If all work is completed, the child could read his or her free reading book, serve as a mentor or tutor to other students, or pursue research on a high-interest topic. There are ways to complete lengthy assignments that could be accomplished with the extra time at the end of each school day. I am certain you would not receive pushback from parents, working outside the home or not. Let school be a true work experience for children, and they will learn the discipline they need to succeed in the real world.

ACTS OF KINDNESS

Memory quilt for a favorite pastor

I shall pass this way but once.
Any kindness I can show to any
human being; Let me do it now.
Let me not defer nor neglect it,
For I shall not pass this way again.
- Etienne De Grellet

Etienne De Grellet, or Stephen Grellet, as he later became, was a prominent French-born American Quaker missionary. Grellet fled France in 1795, during the French Revolution and settled in New Jersey. There, he met and married Rebecca Collins, and served his church faithfully for years as a missionary, advising people in leadership positions in this country.

For nearly thirty years, these famous words by Grellet have haunted me, and motivated, my behavior. It feels as it you don't get a second chance to make a good first impression, so make each action and word count the first time around. That's the message that resonates with me.

While preparing to offer a fond farewell to a beloved pastor in Naperville, Illinois, many years ago, a group of us collaborated on a quilt with a silhouette of a stylized Good Samaritan walking along side a poor and aching man in need. We, somehow, transferred that image to fabric, stitched it to the quilt and added embroidered names of families and friends of this man. At his farewell dinner, while presenting the quilt, I recited the passage from Grellet from memory. When the pastor looked me in the eyes, I realized he was quietly sobbing. Those words struck a chord in his heart. Mine, too.

Throughout life, and within my church, we are constantly challenged to perform works of mercy, and give selflessly of our time, talent, and treasure. Lately, I have come to believe that time is the most precious of all gifts. If there is a way to donate time to a project—to show up and be present—I am most comfortable in that role. The words of Grellet always whisper in my head to do it now and not delay.

Acts of kindness include driving a friend to her chemotherapy treatments, preparing and delivering a meal for a sick neighbor, and knitting scarves for the homeless. My daughters live by these words as well by volunteering their precious time to help at church, lead a Girl Scout troop, and deliver much-needed diapers to a women's homeless shelter in the inner city of Columbus.

Never have the words to stand up and do it now been more important than today. We live in a society that needs selfless helpers to pitch in and assist where the need exists. Do it now. Don't let the moment pass. This moment in time will never come again.

THE REAL GIFT

Most people agree that a baby is a gift from God, one that comes with joys and exhaustion. The first sight of that fresh tiny human with ten fingers and ten toes sends a shiver of delight through our souls as new parents, and makes us smile with both our eyes and our mouths.

The first year is a steep learning curve for inexperienced parents as they learn to master feeding and sleeping schedules in addition to keeping their baby safe and happy. No small task, for sure. The reward for the long, tiring hours of this work is the first toothless smile, presented with great enthusiasm using all the muscles of the baby's body including their tiny flailing arms and legs. Parents and grandparents live for the smiles, the laughs, and the first attempts at words that represent an object or a person such as "Mama" and "Dada," usually the first words out of the mouths of our sweet little angels. Babies know how to engage us so we stay interested in the 24/7 routine of daily care and maintenance of an infant.

Chasing a toddler is an endless mission. They teach us to be swift of foot and hand as we grab and go or intervene in unsafe situations such as careless steps onto a busy street. Stay alert and stay focused, because they are smart and they are fast! My older daughter was known to outrun her good-natured, five-foot tall paternal grandmother and giggle while doing it.

Pre-school children are certainly a joy. Any child who can imagine a princess out of a pile of old clothing or create a flower garden drawing with crayons is a genius in my world. They laugh easily, talk, express their likes and dislikes, and still nap! The afternoon nap is the only break in a typical 14-hour day of continuous care giving and cleaning.

The school years pass quickly and soon your gift of a baby morphs into an adolescent with enormous piles of dirty laundry, a huge appetite, and a messy room to accompany her. The teens most familiar to me are loud with the music they play nonstop. They eat a full refrigerator of food in about three days, and constantly need money. Five dollars for this, two dollars for that, and cash for a new T-shirt for the big game Friday night.

Teen years are challenging for parents. Unless the child is a model student and citizen, things might not turn out as expected. For example, there can be drinking, and smoking. There can be unsavory characters in their world that need to be weeded out. They might refuse to study and prepare for class each day. There could be car accidents along the way. A variety of distractions could impact the life of a teen and her parents at some point. As a parent, stay strong, focused, and rock solid in your convictions about what is right and what is wrong. My main message to my daughters while they were in high school was this: "I am here to protect you. Like it or not, my job is to keep you safe." With clear values coming from home, school, and church, I felt as though we covered the bases of good parenting. Through the years of challenging behavior and some sleepless nights again when my daughters were teenagers, we did manage to come out the other side with a loving, attentive, and respectful relationship.

As young adults, they both privately offered the blanket apology to me at different times that went like this: "Mom, I'm sorry for everything I did in high school to worry you." That simple line felt so good, but here's what I learned from the experience. While the new baby is truly a gift from God, the real gift is the adult child. They become fully formed, and fascinating as adults. They treat me like a friend. And they pay their own bills. God knew what he was doing with parents. He said if you put in the hard work for 21 or 22 years, there is a huge payout for you—the adult child. Best gift ever!

Part Four

MIDDLE YEARS

CHRISTMAS 1991

Joan and Kristina 1991

The year 1991 represented a simpler time for me. Our nuclear family of four all lived under the same roof in Naperville, Illinois. Vito enjoyed his career as a human resources consultant in and around Chicago. I worked locally and part time as a college instructor at North Central College, a few short miles from our home. Kristina thrived as an eighth grader at Saints Peter and Paul Catholic School, also in Naperville and across the street from my employer. Just four years behind her older sister, Anne seemed more grown up as a fourth grader that December.

The preparations for the holiday included the usual round of festive gatherings with friends and neighbors, as well as the numerous Christmas Masses and seasonal programs at church and school. Our home was perpetually fragrant with the aroma of sugar cookies, pumpkin bread, and mulled cider. The holidays sparkled and shone with brilliance. Our little family was happy.

With wish lists for Santa thoughtfully compiled, fantasies of Christmas morning swirled in my daughters' heads. Kristina hoped to unwrap Rollerblades, perfume, a Luke Perry calendar for her room, and a zipper sweatshirt from The GAP, as well as a custom closet from California Closets. Anne's list, much more extensive, included the American Girl Doll Molly McIntyre, the doll's accessories, seven variations of Barbie dolls, candy, hair scrunchies, and a custom closet like her sister.

Every year, we celebrated as we always did with early Christmas Eve Mass followed immediately by a Lithuanian meal comprised of twelve cold meatless dishes in honor of my husband and his heritage. The menu always included pickled herring, cold beet soup, rye bread, and potato salad, a spread hardly touched by our daughters. Borrowing from my family roots, our traditional Christmas Day meal consisted of turkey and all the trimmings, plus more treats and gifts. Holiday music played softly in the house as we opened brightly wrapped presents and enjoyed each other's company.

Today, our daughters have their own families to celebrate with and a combination of traditions they created with their husbands and children. For example, they follow their childhood tradition of early Christmas Eve Mass, followed by a hearty hot meal, and the magic of Christmas morning experienced in their own homes with their own small nuclear families of four. Gifts, toys, hot chocolate, and monkey bread have all made the list of holiday traditions for them.

My wish for the grandchildren as they grow older is the continuation on the path of honoring the Christ Child, celebrating with family, and remembering our loved ones with one special gift, just as the three Wise Men did for Jesus centuries ago. These are still my most treasured traditions, now applied to a modern world.

A LITTLE SOMETHING TO MARK THE PASSAGE OF TIME

Vito, Joan, Kristina, and Anne in Las Vegas

Birthdays represent a clear distinction from one year to the next. That one special day each year has always been viewed with anticipation on my part. I look forward not only to my birthday, but also to the birthdays of my friends and family. The occasion is usually marked by a greeting card with an additional personal message, a treat, and a thoughtful gift selected specially for that person.

In 1962, my parents gifted me with a shiny new bicycle to help me celebrate the demarcation from single to double digits on the scale of years.

The bike meant freedom, independence and mobility. I quickly became a trick rider as I glided effortlessly around the city blocks in my neighborhood without ever touching the handlebars. As a fourth grader, that bike was everything to me and I treated it with love and care—something special to mark the passage of time.

Thirteen is a significant birthday, as well. That is the moment one moves into the teen years. My mother always understood the importance of this birthday both in becoming a teenager and a young woman. Her gift to me in 1965 was a lovely little pearl ring in a gold setting. That ring accompanied me to every school dance, as well as special occasions such as church events and weddings. Today, my older daughter Kristina wears the ring on special occasions and regards it as a treasured gift. Someday, the ring will be presented to Kristina's daughter, Grace, with the story of how it represents the transition to the teen years. The ring was something special to mark the passage of time.

Years later while celebrating my last year as a teenager in 1971, my boyfriend of only a few months who later became my husband surprised me with a bicycle. That gift was especially thoughtful, given the fact that he subsisted on a shoestring budget as a graduate student at Kent State University. In the spring of my freshman year, the warm sunny days were calling us to ride the back roads of Kent and enjoy as much sunshine and warmth as possible after the long, harsh winter in northeast Ohio. Once again, this new and shiny bicycle represented freedom, independence, and something special to mark the passage of time.

Fast forward to the year I turned 50. Unlike some women, I am a female who embraces age and aging. For at least three full years prior, whenever asked about my age, I would happily reply, "I'm almost 50." That milestone birthday was just around the corner.

Not long after every scrap of New Year's confetti was swept away in 2002, I found myself planning a special event. I longed to host a gathering of my closest 20 friends and celebrate, girl-style, with an elegant dinner accompanied by champagne and dessert. Along with my hosting of dinner and drinks for 20, I requested a short paragraph from each guest about her most important life lessons. The wisdom of this group would eventually be compiled into a memory book of the event and the celebration. The evening, the laughter, the friendship, and the wisdom created the most special "something" to mark the passage of time.

Turning 60 is another milestone in a person's life. Even in my wildest dreams I could not have planned something as joyful as dinner at the Eiffel Tower with Kristina. The meal was a feast for both the palate and eyes. My plate sizzled with pan-seared salmon and roasted vegetables. The setting was a dream come true with a dazzling view of Paris at dusk, and the service was equally delightful. Each mouthwatering course was presented by a young man speaking perfect English, along with model good looks. "Wow!" was the only reaction I managed that evening. Truly, that dining experience embodied the something special to mark the passage of time.

Now, I am older and wiser. Currently in my late 60s, I know how to celebrate, how to remember what matters most in life, and how to pace myself. Yes, I can be the responsible adult and the wise mentor to younger people, unless I am dealing with Kristina. Her vision for my 64th birthday was a weekend for four in Las Vegas, with tickets to see Britney Spears in concert at Planet Hollywood Resort and Casino. On April 15th that year, amid thousands of screaming fans, flashing lights, dancing extras, and loud music, I enjoyed a show that lasted 90 minutes. Again, I found myself celebrating the passage of time. Do I feel old? Compared to 30-something Britney fans, yes. Do I mind? No. Am I still in the mood to celebrate? You bet I am.

I will never tire of the way our family celebrates birthdays. Making the day, and week, memorable has always been our mission. Finding that certain something to mark the passage of time will forever be the end goal.

THE YEAR OF SAYING YES

Lambeau Field

My first year in Wisconsin was characterized by change. If you believe current research, change is good. Change means growth. From June 2014 to June 2015, my persona morphed into a cheese-loving, daily walking, Packers super fan. Monumental changes, for sure. With an open heart and an open mind, that time period became my "year of saying yes."

Approximately ten years earlier, when my husband and I were still fully engaged in our careers in eastern Iowa, our grown daughters began the conversation about moving in retirement. The message was always the same—

move to either Columbus or Milwaukee, their hometowns. Apparently, it made no difference where we moved, as long as we moved in retirement to be closer to one of them.

Fair enough.

Time passed, we approached retirement age, and our decision was made. We would leave eastern Iowa, our home for 20 years, and relocate to Milwaukee. That location was only 200 miles from our current home versus 500 to Columbus. The move would be easy and convenient since it was just a three-hour drive and kept us close to Chicago, the residence of my in-laws. Decision made—done and done.

Soon reality washed over us, and we asked ourselves the tough questions. Where do we live? How do we live? Condo or house? Urban or suburban? During a long afternoon of house hunting on the North Shore of Milwaukee on a grey March day, we settled on a house within a two-block walk of our daughter, Anne, and her family in Whitefish Bay. Parks, recreation, church, schools, library, the lakefront and my beloved coffee shops were all within an easy ten-minute walk from the new house. Bingo!

Aside from the inconvenience of a six-month home renovation and a steep learning curve to assimilate Wisconsin culture, including fish fries, football, history, and geography, this has been my "year of saying yes." This one simple response has led me to make new friends, confidently chart unknown waters, and put down roots in my new community in a fairly short amount of time.

Here's an example. The week our furniture arrived by van from Iowa to Wisconsin was stormy and cold, for the third week in June. In spite of the uncomfortable weather, I said "yes" to watching my grandson play T-ball at a local school field. Had I passed on that invitation, I would never have met my new friend, Rose. We are now on the level of lifelong friends. Rose and I meet religiously for coffee dates each week at Panera, and have come to appreciate the blossoming friendship as a blessing. Shivering in the cold while watching four-year-olds relentlessly swing at a ball is the sacrifice one makes to remain open to new opportunities. Rose is my new friend home run!

As a new member of Holy Family Parish, I said "yes" to participating in a women's retreat in November of our first year in town. While on a meal break that Saturday evening, I was approached by a senior church volunteer about cooking fish at the annual Lenten fish fries at church. I would learn that Wisconsin takes its Friday night fish fries very seriously, especially during Lent. Would I prepare the baked fish each Friday in Lent? As I questioned this person who approached me, I was not even clear on how to find the kitchen in the Parish Center nor was I even sure of the procedure used to bake fish. "How many fillets are cooked each week?" "Would I have help?" "What are the hours?"

After some in-depth questioning, I cautiously said "yes." To that one agreement, I am deeply grateful. Each week, my confidence grew as I solo prepared approximately 250 fillets of cod, while baking about 100 potatoes. I mastered the kitchen ovens, the recipe, and the timetable. In the process, I made some delightful new friends in the kitchen. It was a joyful experience and one I hope to repeat in the years to come.

During a mild January weekday, and by mild I mean 30 degrees, my daughter unexpectedly relieved me of my after-school sitter duties for my four-year old grandson. That morning, my husband approached me with the idea of a day trip. "How about driving to Green Bay to see Lambeau Field?"

On a whim I said "yes" and we ventured off to parts unknown for the day. The tour of Lambeau Field was a football lover's dream. Having long been a fan of Aaron Rodgers and his superhuman quarterbacking skills, the sacred space awed me, along with its honored past. As I toured, explored, and listened, only one question came to mind for our guide: "Does Aaron Rodgers actually live in Green Bay?" I got my answer, which was he lives north of the city, along with a souvenir photo on the hallowed grounds of Packer territory. It was a perfect day, and an easy touch down.

Finally, writing class at the local community center over the past year has presented several opportunities to stretch and grow as a writer. I tossed my hat in the ring for a writing competition and actually allowed strangers to read my personal essays and judge them for the first time since high school English class. With a simple "yes" to entering the Waukesha Writers' Contest, I can now call myself an award-winning writer.

That first year flew by with a mix of friendly new faces, day trip destinations, arts and crafts, interesting food, unique experiences, and loads of memories. Did the 12-month time frame evaporate quickly? It certainly did. I am a different person today than I was upon my arrival in Wisconsin.

The people and opportunities in this state have changed my thinking and outlook forever. I owe the kind hearted residents of southeast Wisconsin a debt of gratitude for reaching out to me, and my presence of mind to just "go with it" while discovering where the road leads. The lesson learned in the process was this: start with a smile, trust your instincts, and respond with a confident "yes."

THE ART OF THE COFFEE DATE

Rose and Joan at Panera

Coffee dates—with their ability to enlighten, coach, and entertain us—seemed to become fashionable among ordinary folks and co-workers in the mid-1990s thanks to the television show *Friends*. With Monica, Rachel, Phoebe, Ross, Chandler, and Joey all sitting around Central Perk talking, laughing, and sharing stories, the trend gathered steam in a noticeable way from New York to Los Angeles.

Personally, I have always loved the bar scene with its laughter and frivolity. The tribal behavior of friends, all gathered around drinks and food, has always filled me with joy. Local bars continue to serve as the primary place to meet friends who want to visit, share experiences, laugh, and perhaps shed a tear or two. The concept of neighborhood watering holes is not new, but the updated version of meeting over non-alcoholic beverages in daylight hours appeals to me on many levels.

My experience with coffee dates began in the 1990s with the grand opening of Borders, literally in my own back yard in Davenport, Iowa. From the start, I scheduled meetings with friends and co-workers in the coffee shop for sessions of idea-sharing and information exchanges while savoring the aroma of freshly ground coffee. I'm strictly a tea drinker, but I love the smell of brewed coffee. Our conversations ran the gamut from family drama to work issues to upcoming travel, all while perfecting the art of storytelling. Thousands of stories have been exchanged over the years with friends and work buddies.

In the past, some of my favorite encounters with friends included those dates where I learned about someone's job change and why, someone's love troubles and why, as well as some good old-fashioned truth telling about bosses, in-laws, and ex-friends. The best stories are those that make me laugh from my belly or tear up out of sympathy for the storyteller.

Over the years, I have been privy to vignettes describing the passing of loved ones, mostly our parents, the angst of teenagers, corporate politics, and grandchildrens' humor in all their sweet innocent iterations. From those angelic little voices came sentences such as: "This is so dood" describing an especially delicious meal. Or, "Gwacie, wait for me" when trying to keep up with a very active older sister.

I became a Fort Knox-like vault of information on how parents decline physically, the best interventions for the elderly, and how to honor the wishes of sickly parents. My friends and I shared countless stories with great detail about how one passes from this earth to the next world in the loving arms of family. Lessons from the dying always carry strong messages for the living on how to proceed in life in the absence of that guiding force.

Panera, City Market, and Colectivo all provide a warm, comfortable setting for stories that impact the heart, the mind, and the emotions. We gather strength to put one foot in front of the other, to encourage, to love, and to understand our own role here on Earth. My greatest teachers in life have been my girl friends. I treasure the time spent over drinks while dissecting the latest world news and personal issues. It's no accident these wise women are in my life. Their words carry a profound message that never fails to sink deep into my soul.

Just as the *Friends* cast grew in love and devotion to one another over the course of their run on television with a warm neighborhood coffee shop serving as the backdrop, my life has evolved as well. For me, coffee dates, over the past 20 years have served as the equivalent of a master's degree in psychology. My friends and colleagues all agree at the end of our session that we have, temporarily, solved the world's problems, and that the conversation is to be continued.

LIFE LESSON

Chloe on her 13th Birthday

Of all the jobs I fantasized about as a young girl such as fashion model, mystery novelist, or world traveler for UNICEF, I never imagined I'd be an end-of-life caregiver, ministering to the weak and dying. My story may not be unique among middle-aged women. Many of us find ourselves unofficially recruited for emergency roles we feel unqualified to handle as we learn to make the most of the situation with on-the-job training. Yet somehow, I came to be known as my family's relief when the situation was frighteningly close to the end.

My daughter Anne had always longed to own a small dog she could nurture and love like a child. After several summer jobs and a strict saving plan, she purchased Tinkerbelle, a four-month-old male Yorkshire terrier. Through Anne's fast-tracked years of college and graduate school, Tinkerbelle became her constant companion, licking Anne's face at the crack of dawn to start the day, walking proudly ahead of her on their daily outings, and sleeping under her covers at night for warmth and protection. At only five pounds, Anne's little buddy was as fragile as the wishbone of our Thanksgiving turkey.

With a cross-country move for an exciting new job that required long hours at work, Anne reluctantly turned Tinkerbelle over to me when he was about four years old. While I have always loved dogs, I needed to adjust and restructure my life to accommodate Tinkerbelle due to my own traveling job that took me away from home several 12-hour days each week. So I rounded up all the back-up dog walkers I could find, ranging in age from junior high school to high school and even college girls. Tinkerbelle loved the ladies! Each walker poured affection on our little man, and he relished the attention.

Sadly, in 2008, Tinkerbelle's seventh year, he developed cancerous tumors. Even with the intervention of a well-respected local veterinarian and the assistance of the animal hospital at Iowa's finest university, Tinkerbelle couldn't be saved. As a novice end-of-life caregiver, I followed my instincts daily. I had developed a routine for Tinkerbelle that included hand feeding and watering every three hours, then placing him on the grass on the front lawn just as often and keeping him wrapped in a hand-knit baby blanket the rest of the day.

After Tinkerbelle's passing, I learned that I missed the ritual of caring for him as much as I missed my little companion. That part of the life lesson gradually came into focus for me, though it wouldn't make sense for another few years.

Fast forward just one year in 2009 when I found myself performing the same end-of-life rituals for our other daughter's dog Chloe who had grown up in our home for well over 13 years. Chloe was a black and white female Shih-Tzu we bought for our daughter Kristina when she turned 17 years old in 1995. A puppy was her only birthday request, and my husband felt he owed her a special birthday after moving her to a new state the week of her "sweet sixteen" one year earlier. Immediately, Chloe became my girl. Since I did the house breaking, feeding, watering, and walking, Chloe knew who to follow 24/7. She understood how to snuggle up to me on the couch at night, nuzzling in close to let me pet her while I relaxed at the end of a long, tiring workday. I began to consider Chloe my healer.

As with Tinkerbelle, Chloe also had some cancerous masses that required major surgery to fix. I did think long and hard about the options with the quality of life for her as an elderly dog. In the end, during the final two days with Chloe, I hand fed her dog biscuits and carried her to the lawn every few hours. She, too, needed compassionate end-of-life treatment like Tinkerbelle had received just a year earlier. My role was clearly defined yet again—care for our beloved Chloe and keep her comfortable in her final days. The end arrived late on a Friday afternoon in the vet's office as I stroked and comforted her through the final minutes of life. She died peacefully in my arms, just as Tinkerbelle had done a year before.

One year later in the spring of 2010, I yet again faced more tragic news. My father was in hospice care in a veterans' hospital 600 miles from my home. What do I do? Of course, there were pressing work issues and deadlines. Of course, it would have been more comfortable to leave him in the capable hands of professionals who knew exactly how to care for a human being at the end of life. And still, I felt compelled to travel and be at my father's bedside by noon the very next day. Although he never opened his eyes or spoke a single word in the hours I held vigil at his bedside, he responded by sucking when I swabbed his dry mouth and lips with a cold, wet sponge every hour. As I settled in for the night at his side, holding his hand and waiting, I never thought I would be the last person at my father's side when he took his final breath. The moment happened just before 10 p.m. on a Thursday night in May.

Alone with my father, holding his right hand in mine, and sitting close to the edge of the bed, I suddenly looked up with the realization that he had stopped breathing. Instinctively, I leaned over his right ear and whispered, "I love you, Dad" while stroking his cool cheek. Within minutes, a nurse arrived on the scene to check his vital signs. Although my dad still had a heartbeat, he was losing his body temperature rapidly. It took only a few minutes for his heart to finally stop beating and for him to pass quietly to the other world. It was a calm scene in his dimly lit hospital room that night. Again, another living soul had passed while I gently held on.

How could I be the last person in the room when my father died? How could I be expected to care for sickly pets without an instruction manual? How could I be the sole witness to those life-altering moments? The realization hit me later that I was present for a reason. Now, whenever I recount the story of my father's final day on earth, and how I was there at his bedside when he drifted off, I don't think "why me?" Instead, I think of it as a gift to be present during the transition from life to death. The entire experience changed me. I feel more respect for life and the living, as well as the need to comfort those who may be suffering.

Now, as my husband and I begin those challenging conversations regarding our own final care, he has acknowledged that I will be the one to make his decisions—to be there in the end. I understand the comfort and care he has requested, and he knows my needs, too.

I now view the passing of a loved one, and those quiet moments leading up to it, as a gift given by the sick and dying to be treasured by those left mourning. Life skills combined with life experience have created in me a rebranding of sorts—comforter to the sick and dying. I will never take life and death in a casual way or underestimate the power of unspoken messages from the deathbed. To me, that is the most profound life lesson.

Part Five

GRANDCHILDREN

GRACE'S HEART: 2016

Grace with her big heart

Seven-year-old Grace is kind, happy, and helpful to everyone she meets. In short, Grace is the type of girl you want as your best friend. She remembers to include people and is always quick to inquire about others when they are absent. In the past, Grace has even referred to me, Grammie, as her "really best friend." Grace is my heart.

Grace possesses my heart simply because she has shown me hers. I have witnessed firsthand the gentleness and compassion Grace shows toward her beloved dog, Maggie who is 12—that's 84 in dog years. With a loving and patient approach, Grace walks Maggie around the block each evening after dinner.

Grace is the number one helper at home while setting the table for dinner, putting away her clean clothes, and making her bed each morning before breakfast. In fact, she has recently adopted the Marie Kondo method of organizing her drawers and closet, a real accomplishment for someone her age.

On the school front, Grace participates willingly in each and every assignment, which often includes helping the Japanese students in her classroom who speak very little English. Her attitude in school is every teacher's dream—helpful, attentive, and diligent about producing her best work on all assignments. Grace is always quick to volunteer and help the teacher, a real plus in a full classroom of diverse learners.

As my firstborn grandchild, I could not have asked for a sweeter little person. Grace makes me smile, laugh, and play just like a child. She is always asking me to participate in her activities whether at school, at home, or in Girl Scouts. Now, with her new interest in baking, she is developing a variety of cooking skills to share with me.

On a past coffee date to La Chatelaine in Ohio for afternoon drinks and snacks, I asked Grace to tell me a story that might make me laugh. It was a coffee date, after all, and that's what ladies do when they are together. Grace thought long and hard about this request and finally told me a knock-knock joke. It was funny, silly, and made me smile from the top of my head to the tip of my toes. Again, Grace took her assignment very seriously—making me laugh over a simple afternoon coffee date at our favorite French bistro.

With only one piece of advice going forward to the man who eventually wins Grace's heart, I say, "Be kind, and gentle, and patient with my dear little girl. She's a find, one-of-a-kind, and my best friend. I happily pass this treasured spot in her heart on to you if you are capable of protecting it for the rest of your life." Grace is my heart, and someday, she will belong to someone else. For now, though, I treasure my little Grace and our special relationship that makes me smile, laugh, and love as only Grace can do each time she reveals her heart to the world.

LITTLE SLUGGER: 2018

Luke, our little slugger

Ominous grey puffy pillows of clouds loomed overhead. The Raptors took the field for one last showdown with the team that had defeated them 14 to zero in the regular season. This is Little League in Whitefish Bay, Wisconsin, where the sport of baseball reigns for kids from elementary to high school. This is serious stuff for a kid no bigger than about 53 inches tall and 60 pounds. Luke, our little slugger, is my family's MVP.

As game time rolled around that Saturday afternoon, the temperature hovered in the low 80s with just about as much humidity. It was the kind of day that made spectators sweat through their clothing just by sitting for two hours on lawn chairs. Hot, sticky, and threatening rain—perfect conditions to play ball.

Luke's team did well in the first inning by gaining a run, which proved to be a very exciting start to the game. As the teams progressed through the innings, the Raptors found themselves down nine to two as the sixth and final inning began. With two outs on the scoreboard, our little slugger came to bat, knowing he would be hitting for the last time as a player in the Pee Wee League. Next year, God willing, Luke would join the ranks of the Minor League with player pitches. This year, though, Pee Wees still had the advantage of using a pitching machine. With two teammates on base for the Raptors, he watched carefully, passing on many of the pitches to be certain of just the right one.

Suddenly, we heard the recognizable crack of the bat and the crowd watched as Luke's hit did the most favorable arc possible—landing beyond the fence in outfield. Luke rounded the bases of his homer, bringing in three runs. The screaming began, and his mother tried to catch the event with the camera on her phone. Between slightly bad quality and jerky camera motion (due to his mother's excitement) the choppy video captured the spectacular home run and immediately made its way onto Facebook. Luke's home run bumped the final score to nine to five, still a loss for the Raptors, but it didn't matter a single bit. Luke had achieved something very special that grey afternoon at Craig Counsell Field in Whitefish Bay. He made his last time at bat for the Pee Wee League one of his best hits ever. The crowd cheered, his teammates cheered, and it made for an exciting game for anyone at the field that day.

Our little slugger is a hero, a real student of the game of baseball, practicing with his father most evenings. In the end, I hope his final Pee Wee hit will be indicative of his future baseball endeavors and that he will continue to amaze his fans in the world of Little League for years to come.

ADELINE'S BACKPACK: 2016

Four-year-old Adeline is part tomboy, part princess. Her school backpack reflects her diametrically opposed points of view and style. On a typical school day, there might be an assortment of items ranging from a twig to a fancy headband with a large fluffy pink bow half the size of her head.

The backpack itself is decorated with a variety of pink flowers, cherries, butterflies, and leaves, all in a beautiful array of bouquets and arrangements. Adeline decided on this backpack months ago while school shopping with her cousin Grace, a second grader in the fall of 2016. Even though the girls lived in different states, they were excited to have matching backpacks. Also adorning the exterior is Adeline's collection of animal key chains and stuffed toys along with her miniature bottle of hand sanitizer, because she likes to keep her hands very clean throughout the school day. In addition to the one large inner compartment, there are four additional zipper compartments for smaller items. Clearly, this is the gold standard of backpacks for young girls.

On one particular sunny fall day, I was surprised to find a pink zippered sweatshirt, a red cardigan with a sweet ruffle around the neckline, the enormous pink bow headband, Adeline's hot pink and turquoise lunch kit, as well as a hot pink toy patent leather purse full of "treasures." In addition to the girlie items in the backpack, I discovered a Wilson NFL football with blue and white stitches for tossing around the playground after school. The backpack also included one twig, one white sheet of paper with orange scribbles, two long strips of white paper with Adeline's doodles and drawings, one empty purple plastic school folder, and a wood chip—a diverse collection of items, for sure.

These objects could be the archaeological finds that reveal the clues to Adeline's personality. Truly, there is a yin and a yang to Adeline's authentic self: the football and the dainty pink purse, the wood chip and the bright pink headband, the twig and the ruffled red sweater. Who is the real Adeline?

She is our sweet little K4 student with many interests at the moment. She is as gorgeous as a Madame Alexander doll when dressed and coiffed for church on weekends. However, she is also the little shadow to her older brother Luke when she tries very hard to match him step for step in sports such as football and soccer and other rough and tumble activities.

Adeline is clearly a dichotomy. Part girlie-girl and part tomboy, she is her own person. There is definitely a place for this little powerhouse in our future, and in the world. Can't wait to see where she lands someday.

CHARLIE'S QUESTION: 2016

Charlie and Grammie

Early one evening in the winter, while watching the brainy contestants on *Jeopardy* win big bucks, a Facetime request presented itself on my iPhone from four-year-old Charlie in Ohio. We chatted and talked for a few minutes about this and that, nothing important or urgent at the time.

Within minutes, Charlie presented his question to me. "Grammie, what do you look like?"

I replied, "Well, you can see me on Facetime."

I assumed he was asking a redundant question since the screen was visible to both of us and we know each other quite well. I was completely off base. Charlie meant something different by his question.

"No, Grammie, what are you wearing?"

To that request, I simply scanned my outfit head to toe, with my phone. My standard daily outfit consisted of black stretch leggings, a white tee shirt and a black cardigan sweater. Charlie seemed satisfied, but I offered more. I walked slowly through the rooms on the first floor. Did that satisfy Charlie? I think it did, especially when I showed him his photos in shiny new picture frames on the side table, the ladder shelf, and the dining room built-ins. After covering those three spaces with my phone, I showed Charlie his granddad, reading the newspaper on the soft beige sofa in the library. Charlie lit up when he saw Granddad, and they exchanged greetings.

After sharing my standard daily outfit and after our little show-and-tell session around the house, Charlie turned and ran from the iPad. His interest had quickly pivoted, and Charlie was off to play with Legos and dinosaurs.

He handed over the iPad to his mom, and a conversation with my daughter continued. Everything was right in the world again as Charlie, losing interest in screen time, fell naturally into his rhythm of solo play. Life certainly can be unexpected and delightful from day to day. But, on this occasion, it was especially amusing to find that Charlie had an interest in how I was dressed for a simple Facetime conversation on a nondescript weekday evening in the winter season of that year.

PENNIES FROM HEAVEN

A found penny

Pennies from heaven are a good thing. We find them on the street, in parking lots, and on sidewalks. They bring us joy, elicit a smile, and remind the lucky individual that someone may be watching over them from heaven.

My first encounter with unexpected money happened in New York City in 1957 at the tender age of five. My family visited the Big Apple for Thanksgiving weekend to enjoy the Macy's Thanksgiving Day Parade. As my father and I passed through the revolving door at Macy's department store later that day, I happened to look down and find seven dollars in cash right before my eyes. The wad was stuck in the door, and became my first unexpected windfall, a five-dollar bill plus two singles. Upon my discovery, I handed the money to Dad. He looked it over and pondered the situation. Then, he decided that finding the rightful owner was impossible in a city the size of New York, and he divided the loot—five for himself and two for me.

Years later, my young daughter Anne and I would shop at Jo-Ann Fabrics for material and supplies for homemade clothing, special event outfits, and Halloween costumes. We usually went there bright and early on Monday mornings at ten o'clock. We soon discovered loose change scattered near the fabric store and the discount movie theater, both located in a strip mall in Naperville, Illinois. I assumed teenagers dropped or pitched the loose change from their weekend visits to the movie theater. Anne and I would then take the time to browse for change outside of Jo-Ann Fabrics. To our delight, we gathered overflowing fists full of change on Monday mornings. Anne was also five years old when she became hooked on unexpected cash rewards.

Fast forward to our life in Iowa. Each summer, my girls and I organized a garage sale at home to help turn over the clutter and make space for new items as my daughters matured, and developed new interests. After one especially successful summer garage sale, I offered to take the family out for a pizza dinner as a reward for working exceptionally hard that week. To my surprise and delight, as we parked the car and closed our doors, there in the gutter of the street in filthy flowing rain water, was a ten dollar bill. My largest find to date!

Now, as an older adult, I am even more aware of how pennies (or other bits of currency) are capable of triggering thoughts of loved ones from heaven communicating with us as we walk through our daily routines. On a recent trip to New York City with friends, and 60 years since my first NYC windfall of cash, I uncovered more of the treasured coins I so love to discover in odd places. In total, I found seven coins—one dime, one nickel, and five pennies, all on the streets of Manhattan. Was this my mother's way of saying "Hi" from heaven? I think so. She once lived and attended college in New York City, so this area always held a special place in her heart.

Two years ago, after the weekly Saturday evening Mass at Holy Family Catholic Church, and while worshipers filed out of our sacred space, eight-year-old Luke approached me with a piece of very exciting news.

"Grammie, I found a diamond on the street today!"

"Wow!" I said to match his excitement.

From all my years of spying random cash and change, I wondered how someone is so lucky as to find a diamond on the street on a random Saturday afternoon. By anyone's standards, a diamond is the equivalent of hitting the mother lode of all finds. While my enthusiasm overflowed, Luke remained pleased, but not elated. I wondered what that meant.

As my reaction swelled much farther than a brief pat on the back, questions poured out of me for this little blue-eyed, freckle-nosed grandson. "How did you spot it? What did you do with your new treasure? How will you keep it safe? Is there a rightful owner? Should you try to find him or her?" With my rapid-fire questions and his casual responses, I realized I might have misunderstood Luke's news.

After more questions, the topic began to circle around to the actual treasure—a dime. Mistaking the word dime for diamond was my error. Luke announced his big news because we've discussed the importance of pennies from heaven—those rare and forgotten coins on the ground that indicate someone from above is watching over us here on Earth.

Diamond or dime, it was a rare treat for Luke to add a special piece of currency to his bank account. Thoughts still swirled and speculation remained for the two of us as to which guardian angel could possibly be sending a message on that uneventful sunny Saturday afternoon in our quiet little neighborhood.

Part Six

OLDER & WISER

GATHERED AROUND THE TABLE: THANKSGIVING 2019

The family gathered around the table

Thanksgiving is a sacred holiday to my family, even more so than Christmas or Easter. It's the holiday that gets top billing each year, and the one for which everyone will travel. Thanksgiving holds a place like no other in the hearts and minds of my family.

In 1985, I began hosting Thanksgiving dinner and, by extension, Thanksgiving houseguests, at the still untested age of 33. My family, including Vito, Kristina, and Anne, along with my mother, my father, my father's new wife, my sister, and her family, all gathered around our table in Kingwood, Texas. I remember serving a turkey and side dishes. However, I do believe that my sister and her family must have helped with food. Seemed like a whole lot of mouths to feed. My specialty at the time was apple pie. So if all else failed, at least we had a decent dessert.

Years passed, and our location shifted several times from Texas to Illinois, Iowa, and Wisconsin, but the menu remained intact. We always included roast turkey, stuffing, mashed potatoes, green beans, corn, cranberry sauce, pumpkin bread, and pies. Traditional and filling! We savored those hot dishes; we loaded our plates with seconds and devoured the leftovers. Everyone showed up, everyone enjoyed it, and everyone in our family always had a four-day weekend. Thanksgiving for us is the no-gifts, no-obligation holiday that is strictly about seeing loved ones and enjoying food.

Now, our holiday gathering has settled on the standard group of 13 family members, nine adults and four children. As the turkey roasts all day, filling our home with savory aromas, family gathers to begin "Happy Hour" a full two hours before the meal is served. Cousins run from room to room, preparing to dazzle the adults later with a floorshow of skits, songs, and magic tricks. The day is perfection. Everyone leaves happy, full, and toting their containers of leftovers. As it should be!

As a family, we have always embraced Thanksgiving Day and weekend. My role has been Ring Master for the past 35 years. Now, with pleasure, I pass the baton to Anne, who will host the meal at her home in 2020. It's time for a new generation of cooks to put their stamp on the meal and the hosting. This holiday is a longtime tradition we cherish in my family, begun by my mother in the 1950s and now landing on Anne, my younger daughter who is ready, willing, and able to pass along a day of food and togetherness with as much pleasure (read: anxiety) as any woman in generations past.

ROMEO'S COAT

Joan modeling Romeo's Coat

Romeo, that man-child, lovesick heartthrob to William Shakespeare's Juliet, was more than our family pet. Our pet-child, a whopping 90 pounds of sheepdog, grew fur faster than Bigfoot. We adopted Romeo from an animal shelter in Illinois and watched as he grew in strength and muscle for the first five years of his life. Daily walks were more of a marathon-style workout for my daughters and me. We loved Romeo like our own child and younger sibling.

Twenty years ago while living in Davenport, Iowa, I rose on a daily basis at the still pitch-black hour of 4:45 AM. The quiet early-morning minutes to myself allowed me to shower, dress, style my hair, and eat breakfast before having to walk the beast. The daily morning walk took anywhere from 15 to 30 minutes, which still kept me on track to leave for work promptly at 6:15.

While out on one of our early morning predawn walks, Romeo spooked at a loud truck rumbling down our street. My furry beast bolted, and I lost the leash. In that split-second his panic suddenly raised me high above the pavement, lifted me parallel to the concrete sidewalk, and returned my body to the hard, cold ground in one piece, flat on my back. I landed in a perfectly choreographed position with all my weight evenly distributed still wrapped in my soft grey wool coat with satin lining. All the credit for that safe landing belonged to the well-padded clothing I sported that day.

No injuries, no marks. I quickly retrieved Romeo who showed only a minor interest in my fall, and we returned to the house. All was well on that coal-black frigid winter morning.

Over the years, that grey coat has remained in my closet. I'm not sure why. It still hangs among my lighter weight jackets and I default to it on the most uncomfortably cold days. That coat continues to protect me and keeps me warm in a way no other coat over the years has been able to do. Now, I refer to the soft grey coat as "Romeo's coat."

Although Romeo is long gone, I still wear that coat and remember how well it protected me from a nasty fall on a dark winter's morning. I am also reminded of my mother's lessons to me as a child. She was very clear about caring for my possessions in a way that would make them last a lifetime. Whether Mother was referring to jewelry, books, photographs, money, or clothing, she helped my sisters and me to understand how to take good care of our things.

To this day, I am still caring for Romeo's coat.

DREAMS REALLY DO COME TRUE

Paul McCartney in Concert

James Paul McCartney, singer and songwriter, became my crush on February 9, 1964. Of course, he was older, wealthier, and far more famous, but a sixth-grade girl can dream. That evening, on our black and white television in our tiny TV room, I witnessed along with 73 million other Americans, the phenomenon called The Beatles. The "four lads from Liverpool" performed twice on The Ed Sullivan Show, as my sisters and I listened breathlessly to their performance that Sunday evening.

The setlist included "I Want to Hold Your Hand" and "She Loves You" both favorites of mine at the time. I will never forget the sweet smiles on the faces of Paul, John, George, and Ringo as they played guitars, sang, and shook their smooth dark bobbed hair. These young men, emerging stars, captured the imagination of the girls in the audience as Beatles fans witnessed greatness in the early stages. I still wonder how those girls in the audience scored tickets for that show.

Through the years as I matured from a sixth grader to a junior high school girl, then to a senior in high school, I watched my secret crush evolve as a musician, performer, and song master. The Beatles owned the charts with number one hit after hit between 1964 and 1970. They left a huge hole in my heart out of pure disappointment when the breakup of the group occurred the same year I graduated from high school. No more "Love Me Do," "Hard Day's Night," "Eleanor Rigby," "Hey Jude," or "Let It Be." I was devastated.

I managed to survive my college years by switching my musical tastes to Elton John and James Taylor, but Paul still beat strong in my heart. Fortunately, Paul regrouped and emerged with the band Wings. Surrounded again by enormously talented musicians, McCartney and his band performed equally catchy tunes such as "Band on the Run" and "Live and Let Die." Thank goodness for the sustained talent of my eternal heartthrob.

Fast forward my life 55 years. I am sitting in the Kohl Center in Madison, Wisconsin, with my patient husband of 46 years who has agreed to indulge my passion for Paul McCartney and all things Beatles for this concert. First, let me simply state that Paul was amazing that evening. He performed for three straight hours with no breaks. His setlist was extensive and covered all the hits I longed to hear him play such as "Hard Day's Night," "Baby I'm a Man," "Live and Let Die," and "Hey Jude." My heart beat loud and strong that evening in Madison. The concert was pure magic. The ease of securing tickets electronically, a marvel of modern technology.

In recent years, I have learned a very important life lesson. If you wait, and if you are passionate about your dreams, they may just materialize. Even if you have to wait well over 50 years, you must understand that dreams really do come true.

ADVICE TO MY YOUNGER SELF

4th Grade Joan

Joanie, don't worry, your life will turn out just fine. You are shy and uncertain of things to come and very cautious about people at the tender age of eight. Relax and put yourself out in the world. Make the first move. Smile and introduce yourself to new people. Show confidence. The reward is certainly worth the risk.

Study very hard in school. Always do more than is expected of you. Literally, your whole career will be built on knowledge and experience. Learn as much as you possibly can about your profession, and work longer and harder than any of your colleagues. A strong work ethic will get you far in life.

Wait to travel. Save your money and go when you are a little older because then the travel is that much sweeter. Places like New York, Los Angeles, London, Paris, Rome, Florence, and Vilnius, Lithuania, will have tremendous impact on you when you are a little older and can understand the value of the experience based on a lifetime of learning and growing. Enjoy travel. The opportunities are endless and will open your eyes to new adventures, cultures, food, and ways of seeing the world.

Also, read, read, read! The classroom is not your only vehicle for learning. You are free to enter new worlds on your own through literature and written communication. Focus on nonfiction where you will learn from each and every page of print. Expand your background knowledge of people, places, events, and history. History shapes our understanding of the present. Learn about art, music, and literature from the best writers in the world, both past and present. Learn everything you can and absorb the information like a sponge.

As a young girl, you have your whole life ahead of you. Form your core values such as honesty, dependability, and a strong work ethic early. Be the friend you want to have in return. Always help others in need, to the best of your ability. Fight for your beliefs and be collaborative in the process. In the end, cooperating with others is far superior to competition. Use your divine gifts everyday as you continually remind yourself that you are a child of God.

CONCLUSION

Adeline in training to be a teacher

My life journey has been about teaching and learning. With every new idea, plan, and product, I see growth and change. Scientists believe that we grow and change until the day we die. My intention is to prove that theory.

When I think of my first teacher, my mother, and all she passed along to me in the 35 years we had together, the lessons still resonate loudly today. For example, she was meticulous in regard to dressing, always putting her best foot forward for the public. Her lessons extended to proper behavior, manners, social graces, and hospitality. Mother mastered all things appropriate and gracious.

My teachers in school provided the solid academic framework for learning that allowed me to be an educator later in life. Organizational skills, neatness in all assignments, and punctuality were lessons learned in the classroom from the age of four on. My teachers in grade school were firm but fair, and I thrived in those conditions.

Friends can never be discounted for their genuine heart and soul. They are my lifeline to laughter and learning in an informal fashion. In many ways, my friends have shaped me over the past 40 years as much as teachers, family, and books.

My children and grandchildren have allowed me to use every bit of knowledge and experience gained both in and out of the classroom to solve problems, organize lives, and nurture young minds. They deserve their share of credit for my life lessons and my continual growth, learning, and laughter.

Finally, I want to give a shout out to the next generation of teachers. I like to think my granddaughter Adeline might be among those educators someday. When asked the all-important question, "Adeline, what do you want to be when you grow up?" her response is always consistent. "I want to be a teacher like Mrs. Gehred." Adeline has known for several years that she most likely will pursue education and classroom teaching as her life goal and try to emulate the special qualities of her K4 and K5 teacher. That goal truly encompasses all the kind and caring teachers she has been privileged to know and learn from in her young life. As parents and grandparents, we acknowledge that a good education can change lives, but a good teacher changes everything.

So, to all the teachers, parents, children, and friends, I salute you for your work and your love of learning. I promise to continue to be a student of the game for as long as I am able to put pen to paper, eyes to page, and voice to ideas. This is for you!

ACKNOWLEDGMENTS

Every project of this scope requires assistance. There are several individuals that always come through for me. First, I want to thank my publisher at TEN16 Press, Shannon Ishizaki, for her kind encouragement once again. Shannon paved the path to publishing for me three years ago, and did the same thing this year. Her guidance is invaluable. Along with Shannon, I want to thank the TEN16 staff, those hard working individuals who happily attend to the details of every project.

The unsung hero of any writing project is the editor. I have one of the finest in the area. Denise Guibord Meister has provided clarity to each essay. Sawyer Denison provided grammar expertise as the project progressed. My gratitude is extended to both of them for their much-appreciated time, effort, and talent.

To these friends who allowed me to tell my stories over hot and cold beverages the past 20 years, I owe you so much. Thank you Kathy Kaczmarek, Jeanne Wonio, Bette Seres, and Rose Landgraf.

Finally, to my family—Vito, Kristina, Anne, Andy, Jon, Grace, Luke, Adeline, and Charlie—you are my world and my inspiration. Nothing gets past you and nothing should. This book is for all the times you entertained and enlightened me with your conversational skills, stories, and jokes. I love you.

CPSIA information can be obtained
at www.ICGtesting.com
Printed in the USA
BVHW030721230720
584325BV00004B/6

9 781645 381426